Easy Phonics

Sherry, the Pretty Shrimp

and other stories

X CH SH

4a

by Tapasi De

Illustrated by Suman S. Roy

ABOUT PHONICS

Phonics is the understanding that there is an important relationship between the letters or graphemes of the written language and the individual sounds or phonemes of the spoken language.

A strong knowledge of phonics helps a child considerably to recognize these relationships, to recognize familiar words accurately and automatically, and also "decode" new words. This knowledge substantially improves the reading ability of the child.

In the *Easy Phonics* series, the basic 48 sounds of English have been dealt with through stories. The series is divided into 4 levels with 4 books in each level. Each book contains 2-3 stories based on a particular sound. Colourful illustrations and the repetition of a particular sound ringing through the story make this series absolutely unique!

CONTENTS

1. Xavier Loses Extra Pounds 4
2. Chen and Her Cockroach Friend 10
3. Sherry, the Pretty Shrimp 20

XAVIER LOSES EXTRA POUNDS

X as in FOX/XYLOPHONE

Xavier the ox was a xylophone player in a band. He was very fond of eating. One day Xavier noticed that his belly bulged and his legs had grown thicker.

He had put on a lot of weight! His wife Xantha kept telling him to exercise. However, Xavier paid no attention to her advice. He would eat six butter cookies at a time!

Xavier's legs would pain all the time. His doctor advised him to get an x-ray done. He also said that maybe Xavier's legs pained because he relaxed all the time and did no exercise.

Finally, Xavier decided to join the Oxford gym. Every day, he exercised for many hours. He also gave up butter cookies and started eating xigua. It is a type of watermelon.

Xavier would hit the gym whenever he had extra time. In a month, the results began to show. By Xmas, Xavier had slimmed down. Xantha was very happy with him. “You look so smart!” she crooned.

Words with the 'X' sound

tax	ox	extra	mixer
remix	text	fix	axe
relax	wax	six	box
fax	xerox	xylophone	fox

CHEN AND HER COCKROACH FRIEND

CH as in CHIPS

Chen was a little girl who lived in China. She loved to eat chow mein with her chopsticks. She would have it with chilli sauce.

Chen had a cute pet cat, called Cherry. Chen had found her at the stairs of a church, one Sunday.

Many a time, Chen and Cherry would sit on a bench and listen to the birds chirping. Chen would eat peaches and Cherry would play with butterflies.

One day Chen's parents went out leaving her alone with Cherry. Chen was busy sketching in her sketchbook. Just then, a big brown cockroach appeared.

"Hey you, pretty girl! What's your name?" the cockroach said. Chen looked everywhere. Then she realized that it was the cockroach who was speaking to her!

"You can talk!" Chen exclaimed. Then began a long chit-chat. Since then, the cockroach visited Chen every day. They would sit on the couch and chat for long hours.

One day Chen invited her friends over for lunch. While eating, she told them about her new friend. But no one believed her.

That evening Chen was playing chess with her parents. “Have I told you about my new friend? It’s a cockroach. His name is Chao,” she said to them.

Chen's parents thought it to be her imagination. However, they did not want to hurt their child. So they did not question her. In reality, Chen's new friend was her fancy as she loved insects.

Words with the 'CH' sound

chew	chop	chips	cheer
chain	chalk	choice	chance
chase	cheek	cheat	champ
choose	touch	reach	coach
beach	teach	ditch	lunch

SHERRY, THE PRETTY SHRIMP

SH as in SHIP

Sherry was a beautiful shrimp.
She lived in a cave under the sea.
The cave was near a sunken ship.

Sherry lived all alone and did all the housework by herself. Every morning she dusted the shelves, washed her clothes and took a shower.

She did not like a shabby house, so she polished everything to make it look shiny. In the afternoon, she shopped for household things.

Since Sherry was pretty, she had many suitors. Amongst them was Sherman the shark!

Sherman was very fond of Sherry. He had proposed to her many times. But Sherry had refused Sherman because she was scared of him.

Sherry wanted to marry Sheldon the jellyfish. One day when Sherry was going to a shop to buy a toothbrush, Sherman began to follow her!

At first, Sherry did not realize this due to the darkness all around. But when she switched on her flashlight, she was shocked to see Sherman.

He was right behind her! "If you do not marry me, I will eat you up!" said Sherman. Sherry swam as fast as she could.

Sherman had a flashlight too. He switched it on and it shone through the dark waters. "Sherry, you cannot hide from me! I WILL EAT YOU UP!" he shouted.

Meanwhile, Sherry hid in the dark cave of Sharon the octopus. Now Sharon was very kind-hearted and helpful. She came out of the cave and stood at the door.

When Sherman saw that Sherry had hidden in Sharon's cave, he decided to go back. Sherry thanked Sharon for saving her life and gifted her a beautiful seashell that shimmered in the dark.

Words with the 'SH' sound

fish	wash	splash	brush
shark	shell	share	shed
sheet	crush	shape	shiver
shoe	shirt	shadow	shower
dash	crash	shock	shout
ship	shaft	shift	shovel
shave	shroud	shrink	shrub

LET'S RECALL

1. How many butter cookies would Xavier eat at a time?
2. What advice did Xavier's doctor give him?
3. What is Xigua?
4. Where did Chen live?
5. Where had Chen found her pet cat, Cherry?
6. What appeared before Chen when she was busy sketching?
7. What did Sherry do in the afternoons?
8. Why had Sherry refused to marry Sherman the shark?